The detailed Biography of

Nancy wake:

The White Mouse of The French Resistance

Daily History

Daily History

All rights reserved. No part of this work may be reproduced, distributed or transmitted in any form or by any means, including photocopying, recording, or other electronic or mechanical methods, without the prior written permission of the copyright owner.

Copyright ©Daily history, 2024.

Daily History

TABLE OF CONTENTS

Introduction..5
   The Importance of Nancy Wake's Contributions to History..........................9

Early life and Background 13
   From New Zealand to Australia...............13
   Childhood Moments of Influence 17
   Early Europe Travels and Discoveries.....21

The Dawn of Resistance 27
   Living in France: A Life of Beauty 27
   A Call to Defy 32
   Entering the French Resistance 36

The White Mouse...39
   Resistance Work Begins 39
   Outsmarting the Gestapo 43
   The Missions of Smuggling Secrets in Nazi-Occupied France.................................47

The War Within 53
   Personal Sacrifices and Challenges 53

3
Copyrighted Material.

Daily History

   Love, Loss, and Survival 59
   Betrayal and Courage in the Face of Danger 63
In the Vangard 68
   Organizing Key Operations 68
MAJOR MISSIONS AND MILESTONES IN FIGHTING FOR FREEDOM 74
Nancy's Contribution to D-Day 78
Life After the War 82
   Transitioning from War to Peace 82
   Pursuits in Politics and Public Life 86
   Honors, Awards, and Recognition 90
Later years and death 94
Conclusion 97
Bibliography 101

INTRODUCTION

In the pages of history, some names stand out for their acts, bravery or indomitable spirit. However, others are not so well recognized but their work was just as heroic being viewed by a few who wished to see beyond the obviousness. Nancy Wake is one of such— an extraordinarily fearless woman who changed what would have happened in history but whose name is overshadowed by other great figures of that time.

To know Nancy Wake is to uncover an amazing story of courage that she showed in fighting unimaginable danger in order to free herself and millions others whose names may never be known. She could have grown up thousands of miles away from the battlefields, far from the terrifying events that would engulf the world soon afterwards in her quiet New Zealand/Australian homeland. Yet somehow war's fires reached within her and inspired a deep resolve which propelled her into its very midst making her one of the most fearsome Resistance fighters throughout WWII.

Nancy's story is one of metamorphosis; a lady who confronted fascism's violence directly rather than remain passive. Her path was neither easy nor direct; it had risks that would have broken many people down. But Nancy wasn't like most people. She was a person who couldn't bear any injustice and saw in fighting against tyranny something worth any sacrifice. From sophisticated streets of Paris to treacherous mountains in France where she joined fight against Hitler's Nazi occupation regime; Nancy's journey took different shape.

Famous Gestapo called her "White Mouse" as she continually eluded them only to escape capture by French underground agents too as they continued working together with her on countless missions. Nonetheless, notwithstanding this skilled operative role played by Nancy, she also acted as leader, strategist and symbol for those working with her since they were hopeful about this leader with whom they shared hope for brighter days ahead. She led hundreds into guerrilla warfare, planned sabotage operations that maimed enemy actions and did everything with the bravery of someone more like herself than what her size and appearance exhibited.

Nevertheless, Nancy Wake does not enjoy as much widespread recognition as she deserves despite all her amazing accomplishments. Even though her story is filled with drama and heroism it is not one that can be found in every other classroom or mentioned in every history book. It was a hidden story just like many of those lives that she saved until recently.

The life of Nancy Wake; goes beyond just honoring a single heroine but also pays tribute to countless others who fought in the dark even if their stories are less told but equally significant. Nancy Wake stands out for being one of those women who live by their principles risking everything in an attempt to save others while remaining unknown for too long thus need to be revered by future generations.

As we take a journey into her life we shall find out not only the events that made her legendary but the kind of person she was- an incredibly brave woman, an undiscovered female icon whose tale shall remain memorable forever.

The Importance of Nancy Wake's Contributions to History

Nancy Wake went beyond her work during the Second World War. Her legacy consists of the courage that she had, noncompliance towards dictators and the need for justice, which is still relevant nowadays. She was one of the most resourceful and audacious members of the French resistance who not only played a pivotal role in liberating France but also served as an epitome of what it means to fight for righteousness regardless of any consequences.

In a world which was fast descending into fascist darkness, Nancy wake opted to fight with will power in place of arms and with faith that everyone has a role in securing freedom. Extraordinary bravery marked all aspects of her resistance work from smuggling downed Allied airmen out of

France to leading large scale guerrilla attacks against German forces. All these were proofs for her indomitable spirit and refusal to give up even when they were outnumbered by far.

However, there is more than just military achievement about Nancy Wake. This was evidenced by her breaking gender barriers in war through becoming a leader in male dominated field and showing that courage knows no gender. When women were confined to supporting roles, Nancy insisted on participation instead became part and parcel fighting vanguard . Thus she managed leadership positions where strategic acumen helped bring many successful operations into being; she became source inspiration both for men and women.

Additionally, Nancy's story could be seen as an example of resilience. She faced numerous personal tragedies together with physical hardships throughout her life. It would have been easy for her spirits to break due to the loss of husband, constant threat capture and execution or destruction from her underground activities at least physically speaking. Nevertheless, persistence defined Nancy wake; devotion guided it always without breaking down once. For every difficulty confronted, however insurmountable it seemed for others' living beings she represented hope thus proving that human spirits can defy anything however hard it might seem.

Another proof of the lasting significance of Nancy Wake's contributions can be seen through the way she has impacted future generations. In turn, her once obscure story has been gaining traction and is now an encouraging example of individual agency within a broader historical framework. She reminds us that one person's actions can make a difference—the fact that bravery combined with deep beliefs can change everything.

The legacy of Nancy wake is far-reaching than her activities during war as it implies core characteristics about courage, leadership, and justice which are timeless. By honoring Nancy Wake, we appreciate not only an extraordinary woman, but also underline the importance of resisting any forms oppression. Such life is so inspiring for everyone who reads it urging them to rise in arms in order to protect freedom which was bravely held up by her.

EARLY LIFE AND BACKGROUND

From New Zealand to Australia

Nancy Wake's story began in the calm, unassuming landscapes of New Zealand far from the chaos and confusion that would later befall her life. Nancy Grace Augusta Wake was born on August 30, 1912, in Wellington, New Zealand, where she was the youngest of six children in a family of humble origins. Her early years were molded by the simple joys and trials associated with growing up in a large closely-knit family. But this period also became the foundation for an exceptional woman who acquired self-reliance, fortitude as well as adventurous spirit which eventually led her into accomplishing extraordinary achievements.

Daily History

At two-years-old Nancy moved with her parents to Australia where they settled down at North Sydney. This marked a new beginning for her as she grew up in a country totally different from that of her birth. Nancy's childhood and teenage life were played out against the vast expanses of Australian countryside steeped in pioneering traditions. It was there amidst vibrant aspects but harsh realities of Australian life that Nancy's character took shape.

When their father left his wife shortly after taking them to Australia, it had a lasting impact on Nancy even after many years later. The Wakes experienced great hardships having been forsaken by their own protector and breadwinner. Her mother who was deeply religious struggled to make ends meet during these moments when they experienced adversity which definitely influenced how Nancy saw things happening around her back, then shaped Nancy's world outlook. This particular situation made sure that she did not have faith on anybody else

Copyrighted Material.

but herself thus creating one of those traits which characterized her throughout life.

She passed through Sydney during early years when she went to North Sydney Household Arts School for some elementary education studies. While being highly intelligent learner, Nancy had never been comfortable with settling for anything less than what was expected from here by society or environment around, such conditions surrounding her. This restlessness combined with a growing desire for freedom led the young girl to leave home at the age of sixteen. Nancy saved a small fortune that she received from his aunt and together with it she decided to start life anew.

As a teenager seeking her niche, Nancy traversed through many adventurous situations and missteps in Australia. By working as everything from nursing aide to journalist, Nancy was exposed to all challenges and successes inherent in a world still controlled by traditional gender norms.

These experiences helped expand her horizons and increased her motivation to get out of an unfulfilling lifestyle.

This longing turned out indeed into something bigger than just herself when Nancy arrived in Europe where she became involved in major conflicts of the twentieth century. However, it was during these early years spent in New Zealand and Australia that the grounds of her bravery as well as determination were laid. The situations encountered; forced independence; developed resilience made this woman to be one of those people who would be remembered as heroic fighters against tyranny after so many years and generations have passed by since then.

To understand the roots of Nancy Wake, we need to look at her early years and how she developed a determination to be above her birth conditions. Moving from NZ's calm beaches to vibrant cities in Australia was only one limb of the journey that would see her traverse history itself.

Childhood Moments of Influence

The experiences Nancy Wake had in her childhood would later shape the kind of woman she became by making her strong willed, independent and resolute. Born into a world that was full of limitations in many aspects, Nancy learned at an early age that overcoming one's circumstances required determination and bravery.

One major event marked Nancy's earlier days; the sudden departure of her father from the family. When Nancy was still a small girl, their dad abandoned them shortly after moving from New Zealand to Australia hence leaving six children for their mum to raise alone. This specific incident defined Nancy as a person. She grieved over her dad's loss and this experience has continued to haunt her till now whereby she understands that life is so unstable and can never be felt secure.

Her mother on the other hand was a strict woman who believed in religion more than anything else. However, even as a young child, Nancy was not easy to control when it comes to following rules. Often they were at odds with each other, refusing such regimentation. What motivated this response was not just defiance but rather an embryonic independence which later propelled her towards outstanding feats of bravery and resistance.

Nancy's early exposure to literature and reading also constituted another decisive moment in her life during this stage. Even though money problems were very serious with her family, she found solace and inspiration out of books. Her imagination got caught up by stories about adventuresome people living faraway lands among others which made it grow restless within itself yearning for escape from the boundaries restricting it back Australia. Subsequently these stories made Nancy start thinking about something beyond what is normal life such as having own decisions or even choosing path.

Resilience had been tested through personal challenges throughout most part of Nancy's initial years while growing up. At some point while growing up as a little girl she experienced some form prejudice due to social class differences that existed then. Being from a poor background, Nancy was very much aware of the class discrimination that separated her from her wealthier friends. Rather than allowing this to feed bitterness into her life, she seized upon these experiences as an opportunity to prove herself. As a result of such encounters, Nancy became hardened and sharp-tongued and thus she developed skills for surviving in societies using both sweet talking and aggressiveness.

One pivotal moment transpired at the age of just eight years when Nancy ran away from home, attempting to live an adventurous existence. Even though this move did not last long, it indicated how much she wanted to have her own freedom instead of living under the expectations of others. This early defiance was an initial step towards the daring acts she would engage in later in life against Nazis' dictatorship.

The moments in Nancy Wake's childhood that signified loss, rebellion and the yearning for something else were her character's foundation. They created the resilience within her as well as an independent spirit which typified her latter life. The origin of Nancy's unshakable determination and strong-willed dedication to freedom at any cost can be traced back to these momentous occurrences.

Early Europe Travels and Discoveries

By the time Nancy Wake reached the end of her teens, she had become even more restless than she was during her childhood. She no longer felt satisfied living in Australia after seeing all its familiar landscapes and following social conventions that were born there. The ambition that possessed her made her wish for a life full of adventure which would take her away from everything she knew so well. This created a wish in her heart to go to Europe; an exciting but unpredictable land where she changed the direction of her life forever.

Nancy set sail for Europe in 1932 with a tiny inheritance from a favorite aunt and an insatiable hunger for something new. Just twenty years old then but never wavering in wanting to discover herself. Stepping on European ground brought about an instant attachment between Nancy and the rich history, diverse culture, and difference in this continent. The enthusiasm and glamour associated with cities such as London and Paris fascinated Nancy as every street seemed to hum with the possibilities of a life less ordinary

Nancy's early years in Europe were marked by a series of travels and discoveries that would shape her worldview and prepare her for the challenges that lay ahead. In London, she immersed herself in the fast-paced world of journalism, taking on various assignments that allowed her to explore the intricacies of European society. Her natural curiosity led to becoming one of those journalists desired by many media houses at will; it didn't take long before she found herself back again at Paris -her second home.

Paris during the 1930s was an example of contradictions, a fountainhead of art, culture, and intellectualism while political upheavals darkened it too. The city's pulsating life fascinated Nancy greatly so much so she spent much time mingling with

Daily History

artists, writers, intellectuals who defied traditional wisdoms through their work.. This exposure to different perspectives broadened Nancy's horizons, deepening her understanding of the complexities of human nature and the fragile balance of power that governed nations.

It was during these early years in Europe that Nancy began to develop a keen awareness of the political tensions that were brewing across the continent. Nancy as a journalist reported on fascism slowly rising, an eye witness to despotic leaders like Adolf Hitler and Benito Mussolini. Her growing interest in their brutal realities made her feel all the more she should do something about them. Nancy's journalistic experiences showed her how much people living under oppressive governments suffered, thus leaving her with no other option but to contribute towards making things different through applying what she had learnt in college.

Nancy also went beyond visiting major cities such as Rome or Paris. She visited Spain and Italy where she saw real poverty and political corruption for herself. These experiences further solidified her belief that the fight against fascism was not just a political struggle, but a moral one. Europe's beauty and sophistication aside; it is still ridden by age-old injustices too obvious to ignore.

Nancy's journeys in 1937 took her to Vienna, a city that was about to be swallowed by the Nazi regime. Here, she witnessed the horror and dread that was beginning to grip the Jews as Hitler's influence spread. For Nancy, it was an experience that would fuel her determination to fight against hatreds and tyranny.

By the time she returned to Paris, Nancy had become a different person from the young ignorant girl who had come to Europe only several years back. Her trips and discoveries have turned her into a passionate individual who is aware of what he talks about; ready to face whatever lay in front of her way. Europe called and Nancy Wake accepted, ushering in this way an extraordinary life of resistance and heroism.

Daily History

THE DAWN OF RESISTANCE

Living in France: A Life of Beauty

When Nancy Wake first came to France in the last years of the 1930s, she was caught by its appeal, culture and sophistication. And especially Paris with its lively art scene, crowded cafes and history rich city promised her life full of elegance and thrill which she had been searching for such a long time. After travelling around Europe for a few years, she had found somewhere that felt like home, a place where she could indulge herself in all the finer things in life while still working as a journalist.

Nancy easily adapted to the French way of life, seizing the opportunities that come along when one resides in one of world's most glamorous cities. She was frequently seen rubbing shoulders with artists, intellectuals and socialites at glitzy parties or dining at some of the best restaurants within Paris. Her natural attractiveness, engaging personality and quick wittedness made her popular amongst this group. It was an existence filled with refinement and luxury far removed from childhood struggles or sorrows witnessed during her travels.

Nancy's life took a major turn in 1939 when she met Henri Fiocca, an affluent industrialist from Marseille who had great charm. Nancy also reciprocated his feelings immediately; hence they became emotionally attached very quickly within no time since they started dating. In 1940 having married they moved to Marseille where Nancy led an opulent lifestyle as wife to a prominent businessman.

In Marseille, Nancy lived like Cinderella. They stayed in an attractive mansion house together with Henri fully enjoying everything that French society could provide them with; they happened to be flying abroad regularly. Henri provided what seemed like perfect partnership as he allowed his independent-minded wife pursue her goals whilst treating her opinions with respect. It appeared for some time that Nancy had struck the ideal balance between love, adventure and interests.

However, even though she was basking in the pleasures of her new life, Nancy could not fail to sense the disturbing changes that were taking place all around her. The world was on the verge of war, and fascism's rise had become difficult to overlook. Nancy knew that even though she appeared well off politically, these differences in Europe were still within her sight. Her profession as a journalist had introduced her to the horrors of Hitler's regime, thus indicating how bad things had become.

As France edged towards war, Nancy became more and more uneasy. She saw what was happening in countries around them due to German occupation and it started to look like a real threat for France too. Although living comfortably in Marseilles, Nancy now felt an increasing urge to act – anything – to prevent the spread of fascism from spreading further. She realized she could no longer sit back and watch millions of innocent people suffer under Hitler's or Mussolini's gruesome regimes stuck in their lives.

Nancy's life of luxury in France was getting increasingly hard to reconcile with the realities of the world she lived in. Although Nancy enjoyed all the privileges that came along with being married to Henri, she couldn't help but notice the suffering that other people were going through. She could not ignore her conscience since it reminded her of deplorable unfairness and hence felt deeply bound by moral responsibility.

That is when Nancy acknowledged that she had made a decision which would have lasting effects on her life. Despite the dangers, Nancy would use her position and resources in fighting against Nazi occupation. Her splendid existence would change into one fraught with peril, resistance and supreme bravery. Nancy Wake was soon to become one of the most dreaded names in freedom's battle as a socialite and journalist herself.

A Call to Defy

Europe spent the end of 1930s being shadowed by this ominous rise of fascism. The threat was not some far away worry but a present danger for Nancy Wake, who had witnessed the horrors of Nazi power while travelling and working as a journalist. The darkness that spread across Europe was beginning to encroach on her life in France with her beloved husband Henri.

Europe, France included, was overshadowed by the shadow of fascism. When World War II broke out in 1939, it did not take long before Nazi Germany targeted French territory. June 1940 saw the unthinkable happening; France had been conquered by German forces and what once used to be a liberal and vibrant nation came under occupation. The speed and violence of German invasion left French people stunned. They weren't prepared for it hence they were crushed by the sheer power of Nazi's war machine.

Daily History

The occupation in France felt like an assault on Nancy's person. A regime she hated had taken over a country that she adored so much. It dismantled bit by bit all that she knew about existence where elegance, freedom, and joy coexisted together whereas fascistic powers took control over them one after another. Living under occupation meant harshness, where restrictions became normalcy; fear always prevailed while Germans soldiers occupied their streets constantly.

However, even when fascism threatened its dark grip on France's streets, Nancy's heart continued burning brightly with hope. These injustices were glaringly obvious to her eyes motivating her strong desire to resist back against oppressive measures that gripped her new home country fiercely. She could not watch as Nazis dictated other people's lives in France without reacting against such evil tyranny that made no sense at all to her soul deep inside compelling her into action.

Copyrighted Material.

Nancy made up her mind about joining the resistance only after deep thoughts about it first knowing quite well how dangerous this might be i.e. she knew she could be captured, tortured and executed. However, the call to defy was louder than her fears. Such actions also included the fact that Nazi did horrible things while innocent people suffered and their freedoms were taken away from them making it look like a worthwhile cause which had been carried forward by Nancy herself. She could not imagine living in a world where such wickedness remained unchallenged.

Her resistance work began with small but very significant acts of defiance. Social contacts were used to gather information which assisted Allied soldiers and downed pilots escape from occupied France. It is through these connections that Nancy's involvement in the resistance began, which shortly became deeper and deeper into her life. Her experience as a journalist came in handy for many reasons especially because she needed to think fast always, utilize all available resources, while remaining focused on accomplishing her primary goal.

The stakes get higher for Nancy the more she delves into the resistance. Her life was overshadowed by fascism for a long time but it made her even more resolute. She understood that the war against Nazis was not only about France but also humanity as a whole. The call to defy had awakened within her an unknown courage and she could sacrifice everything to respond to that call.

Such frivolities were no longer possible for Nancy Wake because fascism had become a concrete reality in her life. This woman, once used to elegance and privilege, was now single-mindedly fighting for freedom as never before. A journey from socialite to resistance heroine started being led by the unrepentant commitment of defying tyranny and restoring freedoms stolen from the people of France.

Entering the French Resistance

Nancy Wake's decision to join the French Resistance was a turning point in her life. As France came under tighter Nazi control, Nancy realized she could not idly stand by. Her conscience and sense of fairness led her to act and she resolved to play a part in the struggle against dictatorship.

For Nancy, joining the resistance began with minor acts of rebellion. She utilized her charm and connections to acquire secret information that she passed on subtly to disruptors within the Nazi leadership. The army of resistance found out quickly that her resourcefulness and audacity made her an asset worth keeping, hence involving herself soon after in what became known as "Pat O'Leary Line", an underground route helping British soldiers and airmen escape capture by Nazis. This scheme depended on Nancy for its success because it required facilities for hiding people temporarily, ensuring their transport via dangerous routes, as well as guidance towards freedom.

As Nancy's involvement deepened, she attracted attention from the British Special Operations Executive (SOE) – an organization dedicated to waging sabotage and spying wars behind enemy lines. The SOE saw her potential and trained her in guerrilla warfare skills including using guns and radios. Quick thinking characterized by remarkable strength even made Nancy one other when compared with many since he got assigned progressively challenging missions.

Bravery and originality distinguished Nancy's contribution to French Resistance fighter's activities during this period. She was admired because of her ability to play German officers or their diversified counterparts using intelligence tricks leading them away from themselves when chasing after here. Beyond gathering intelligence, she coordinated sabotage operations targeting supply lines supporting Germans during

World War II; these moves hampered the military efforts undertaken by Adolf Hitler led regime.

She had played such a central role that Gestapo put $5 million bounty on Wake's head in 1943 considering her one of most effective operatives among rebels'. Regardless of the ever-increasing risks, she never wavered but instead continued with her work under these harrowing conditions leading many people calling her "The White Mouse" as she managed to keep out of the hands of the enemy.

Nancy Wake's involvement in French Resistance was a journey that would shape her into a formidable force against tyranny. By her bravery, innovativeness and unwavering dedication to their cause, she became an iconic figure of resistance and a light amidst one of the darkest chapters in history.

THE WHITE MOUSE

Resistance Work Begins

It was this commitment to the French Resistance that ushered Nancy Wake into a new life, one characterized by extraordinary bravery, deceit and an unbridled sense of fair play. As German occupation of France tightened its grip, so did Nancy's determination. She had already demonstrated courage and resourcefulness in helping allied soldiers escape but now, her resistance work was about to take on a completely different dimension.

Nancy became an important figure within the resistance due to her quick thinking and adaptability. Her activities started in earnest as she gathered intelligence, identified strategic points for attacks and coordinated sabotage against the Nazis. This was no easy task with enemy forces and collaborators all over the place. Nevertheless, through nimbleness and daring blended with seductiveness she outwitted many others who would have tried it.

Nancy proved over time that she was a tough operator as her missions became more complex. She saw to it that essential supplies were transported from one end to another; arranged for secret meetings between agents while also passing crucial information to Allied armies. Her ability to fit into any ecosystem from high society parties all the way down into dark undergrounds of fighters made her most valuable.

Among Nancy's earliest major contributions were sabotage assignments meant to interfere with German supply chains and communication lines. These were dangerous missions which required delicate planning but Nancy's exceptional leadership qualities plus unwavering concentration ensured success at every turn. In every instance when trains derailed or bridges collapsed or vital routes blocked off, she led from the front influencing those around her.

The growing influence of Nancy within the resistance movement soon attracted attention from Gestapo agents whose main aim now was capturing her alive at all costs because they knew what they were dealing with. But again and again Nancy slipped through their fingers earning herself a nickname "The White Mouse" since she had become elusive like such animals during capture attempts by them. With each failed attempt, the Gestapo's anger only strengthened Nancy's resolve as she continued to outwit them.

However, Nancy never lost her nerve despite the ever-present risk. But for her it was not just a collection of tasks; rather this was a personal struggle against tyranny that had overtaken her beloved France. It meant that every successful operation or Nazi plan thwarted took her one step closer to freeing

Daily History

the motherland. Each time she won, Nancy became more and more of a legend.

Nancy Wake's representation as "The White Mouse" demonstrated her indomitable spirit and ingenuity. Her resistance work comprised something greater than fighting Nazis—it symbolized a fight for freedom, fairness and what she believes in. As increased stakes and threats loomed larger, Nancy still rose to the occasion thereby solidifying herself among the most exceptional characters in French history.

Outsmarting the Gestapo

As she became more involved in the French Resistance, the determination of the Gestapo to capture her grew. Her audacious acts of sabotage, intelligence gathering, and support for Allied soldiers had made her a high-value target. Among all other operatives in occupied France who were operated on by Gestapo which was known for its ruthlessness, they considered Nancy as one of the most dangerous. Yet she always managed to outwit them despite their best efforts and this is why she became "The White Mouse."

But Nancy was not just lucky; rather, she had keen instincts that helped her to avoid being captured by enemies quickly. She has an uncanny ability to blend in with different surroundings by changing disguises so often; she might also alter her appearance or even use charm to make people's mind change about her guilt. This is how it came about that chasing after Nancy was like running after a shadow for the Gestapo.

One of these instances took place when Nancy was almost caught by the Gestapo at Marseilles. With all her networks compromised, she got away from this city immediately thereafter. In spite of an intense search operation mounted against her, she passed through many checkpoints without being noticed because of courageously deceptive methods adopted by herself including altering appearances as well as disappearing acutely in time and space while relying on trusted contacts to stay ahead only once such incident arose remaining as ever resourceful though very close to death.

Nancy had another narrow escape during a mission where she and others were nearly caught up with German soldiers. She warded off danger by arguing herself out of harm's way making them believe that they were mere innocent travelers about whom nothing should be done; hence there was no apprehension needed at all. It was a dangerous game plan but worked out perfectly fine since they accomplished their objectives undetected throughout Germany still feeling extremely confident that this incident would discourage them as they proceeded with their war against Nazis.

In addition, the ability of Nancy to defeat Gestapos was also a result of her comprehensive planning. She always looked forward to her possible betrayal or discovery and she had many escape routes and alternative steps. This way she stayed ahead of the Gestapo's moves in trying to trap her which turned into an endless game of cat and mouse that saw them lose time after time.

Nancy was clearly a thorn in the flesh for Gestapo. A reward was offered for her head; her photograph widely circulated; even suspected members at times were subjected to torture by Gestapos as an intensification measure. But Nancy kept on escaping from their grip repeatedly. Her escape abilities became legendary inspiring all fellow fighters while demoralizing the enemy.

Nevertheless, Nancy never lost heart even though she was constantly in great danger. She knew that every day spent freely meant one more opportunity to fight for freedom. Through all odds she defied as a symbol of hope and resilience among those who fought along side with her. Consequently, Nancy's personal triumph over the inability of any German soldier to arrest her signified not only herself but also entire resistance movement winning over Nazis by remaining elusive throughout that period without capture.

The Gestapo's inability to catch Nancy Wake was due to a mixture of intellectual prowess, bravery, and unflinching determination to fight for liberty. She did not manage to avoid being caught simply because she wanted to survive but rather so as not to stop struggling against suppression. Known as "The White Mouse," Nancy became an eternal legend of resistance who the Gestapo could never apprehend at any cost. Her escape tale is one of the most extraordinary episodes in the annals of French Resistance that exemplifies the unbeatable zeal of a woman who would not give up.

The Missions of Smuggling Secrets in Nazi-Occupied France

Nancy Wake's work as a resistance fighter in the heartland of Nazi-occupied France was both highly risky and critical. Undercover smuggling of secrets among her many functions was one of the most hazardous and urgent. Nancy later became a skilled transporter of vital information, documents and supplies for Allied war activities because she had a sharp brain, fearless character and an uncanny ability to adapt to any given situation.

Working under constant threat of exposure necessitated careful planning and strong nerves on Nancy's part in order for her missions to succeed. She was always playing with high stakes since even minor errors could lead to arrests, tortures or deaths. However, Nancy went on with her tasks without even flinching although she knew very well that those secret assignments had potential risks attached to them. She was aware that the intelligence she transported could save thousands of lives from being wasted by the enemy, hence sometimes she lost faith in herself.

Among other things, Nancy regularly transported secret messages and intelligence between different French underground cells and Allied contacts. Many times these included crossing heavily fortified frontiers or passing through numerous Gestapo barriers. To circumvent detection, Nancy used several disguises as well as false identities that would not be easily found out by anyone who looked at her critically. Whether appearing like an ordinary French woman resident, a messenger boy or German informer it did not matter since all these were means to an end in completing her assignments effectively.

Often enough though, the information which Nancy smuggled was concealed in ingenious ways. Microfilms would be tucked away into everyday items like matchboxes or lipstick holders while essential papers were stitched into garments. Nancy had to remain calm under pressure throughout this operation so any signs of nervousness would attract attention. She understood French fluently just like any local resident due to long periods spent within France. With this knowledge she safely accomplished so successful dangerous trips.

In one particularly nerve-wracking mission, Nancy had to smuggle radio codes and plans for upcoming acts of sabotage to a remote resistance group. She had to navigate through Nazi-occupied areas while avoiding the Gestapo and their collaborators. With Nazi patrols on high alert, Nancy's mission was fraught with danger. Still, she managed to deliver this vital information without being detected; hence the resistance's sabotage efforts went uninterrupted. The success of this mission not only demonstrated Nancy's extraordinary skill and courage but also solidified her reputation as one of the most effective operatives in the resistance movement.

Apart from smuggling intelligence, Nancy also played a crucial role in distributing weapons, explosives, and other supplies among various partisan groups. These objects were necessary for destroying German army units or infrastructure. She could not afford to be careless when carrying such dangerous items. Nancy would often travel at night using side roads or hidden paths so as not to be seen by anyone who might report her. Deep knowledge about every corner of France combined with resourcefulness once again helped her successfully supply them despite continuous threats of ambush or betrayal.

On several occasions, Nancy led a band of freedom fighters through hazardous terrain with the aim of avoiding capture. These journeys were usually tough treks across forests, mountains or rivers. Such was the physical and mental strain involved that it never stopped Nancy from dedicating herself totally. Their experience underlined her as a person who inspired others knowing that she will held steadfastly against Hitler's regime forever because she was a true leader when they needed help on how to fight back against Germans who occupied their country.

The reasons for success in Nancy's smuggling missions were not just her guts but also the ability of quick thinking. Her uncanny gift for predicting dangers and avoiding them was amazing. Whether it entailed fake documents, bribing officials or outwitting German patrols, Nancy's cleverness invariably stayed a step ahead of the enemy. It is this quality that helped her carry out many successful operations.

Daily History

Nancy Wake: The White Mouse had to engage in smuggling secrets across Nazi-occupied France, a realm of courage, intelligence and resourcefulness. In other words, each mission was aimed directly at subduing the Nazis' influence over France and preparing grounds for its future liberation. Moreover, Nancy's role as a resistance fighter not only made valuable contributions to allied successes during WW2 but also became an emblematic gesture of rebellion against tyranny. Finally still having a legacy left behind counts as an ample proof of how much one person can achieve regardless of hurdle put on his way.

THE WAR WITHIN

Personal Sacrifices and Challenges

While fighting the Nazi war, Nancy Wake found herself in a similar struggle, an internal one whose significant consequences meant personal sacrifices and continuous challenges. However, freedom struggle required the supreme sacrifice from its participants, thus forcing Nancy as well as many others to make decisions that would forever alter their lives.

For Nancy, living as a guerrilla was very difficult but her emotions were probably the hardest thing she had to bear. Each day reminded her of people she left behind and life which existed before; it was filled with love, laughter and simple pleasures of peace. But all this seemed like ages ago while the harsh realities of war surrounded them. Her responsibilities became too heavy for her to carry around, fear of capture set in; She felt lonely with no shoulder to lean on. This was not what she wanted but it could not be helped. Failure was costly than anything else because much more serious things than what she really wanted were at stake.

One of the hardest choices that Nancy had to make involved abandoning Henri Fiocca her husband behind. Even though they loved each other so much he eventually realized that staying back in France would be perilous for him when Gestapo's grip tightened around her. It did not come easily but with heavy heart she resolved painfully knowing that maybe never will they meet again henceforth again as long as she is alive or dead? That pain lingered long after its cause was gone thus having served as an ever-present reminder which showed how much it cost her personal commitment towards resistance.

Daily History

The physical and emotional impact of this job took a toll on Nancy over time because sometimes there were days when food shortage became frequent leading to hunger pangs and fatigue with every step being fatal if captured by an enemy. Always watchful over her shoulder since no one could be wholly trusted, constantly shifting positions so as not to remain exposed characterized most part of her life. The heaviness sometimes seemed overwhelming; fear and doubt would almost drown her. Nevertheless, she never gave up even when in the darkest moments that came Nancy always found an inner strength within herself to keep going on. She drew her inspiration from many others who were making similar sacrifices like common people risking their lives in defiance of oppressive governments.

The war exposed Nancy to intense human suffering. The whole area was now a place where innocent lives were being lost, entire communities destroyed and France felt a pervasive feeling of hopelessness as it lay under occupation. Her resolve hardened but empathy became deeper over such experiences. That resistance against Nazi Germany was not only about military struggle but also an ethical one too was clear by then because every smallest form of defiance acted as a light amid the dark engulfing Europe.

As a result of this, Nancy's personal sacrifices extended far beyond her own health and mental state. Some of them were taken prisoners or killed in the war field leaving her with no other alternative but to mourn for them. She took every death as a personal loss and as an example of just how high the cost of resistance was. The sense of grief that she had became worse because there were only few times available for mourning. During the war she never stopped, continued fighting despite everything it demanded.

She also experienced doubts throughout all these challenges. At such times she wondered if her endeavors would be fruitless; whether what they gave up their lives for would eventually lead to triumphs. However, in those moments of wavering hope, she drew strength from knowing that their cause was right believing firmly in unwavering righteousness. For instance, against Nazis, Nancy fought an internal struggle within herself based on fear, doubt as well as despair.

The various challenges and personal sacrifices made by Nancy Wake during the war spoke volumes about her very strong personality. Her job left her emotionally drained; she lost friends who died in active service while the pressure to perform was relentless and unending; however, Nancy did not give up at any point in time. Instead she realized that courage did not mean lack of fear but going ahead in its face regardless. Just like on battlefield so too was inwards seen when fighting against oneself: yet amid all these battles Nancy stood firm with an absolute conviction that freedom's fight could be paid by anything.

Love, Loss, and Survival

Amid war's shadowing, Nancy Wake's odyssey was not only one of resistance and valor but also a soulful testament to the complexities of love, loss and survival. These elements were woven together in her experiences and gave impetus to her tenacity at the darkest hours.

Her love for Henri Fiocca was very important to Nancy. This relationship was a beacon of normalcy and warmth amidst the turmoil that characterized wartime. But when she made that heart-rending choice to leave Henri behind, it was done out of necessity. She decided that if she stayed with him, they will all be killed by enemies. It wasn't simply his absence physically; it ripped at her emotionally. The unanswered question about what happened with him combined with regrets of having deserted him and desire for his presence kept torturing her mind. Every victory in her missions was sour since she missed the man who acted as a source of strength and love during this period.

The pain involved in separation coupled up with lost friends and comrades became too much for them to bear. The partisans were like members of family tied together by common interest hence their losses which ranged from getting caught or being killed were extremely painful experiences for Nancy. Each death reminded them how much they paid in their fight against oppressors since every name mentioned meant someone related personally to those moaning deaths while everyone who died fought valiantly against those threats to life. Their sacrifice weighed down on their souls always reminding them about how fragile life is keeping them alert not to lose everything so dearly fought.

To survive in such a dangerous setting took more than mere physical stamina; an emotional fortitude like what Nancy had exemplified mattered a lot too. Her ability as a survivor depended upon constant danger, evading capture round the clock besides the unrelenting pressure to "succeed" on her missions. Nancy's resilience in this regard was a testament to the strength of her heart. She found courage and refusal from within to keep going, taking on her cause and the lost ones who have been as motivations.

The fight for life was not individual; it took place together with other resistance fighters. The comradeship that emerged during times of adversity served both as a comfort zone and a reminder of what they were risking. They faced war's horrors and threats of being caught together hence they could console each other or help escape during moments like these. Maintaining morale among others and nurturing hope amidst tumult would not have been easy without Nancy's leadership, which was also boosted by comforting words she gave to many.

At quiet contemplative moments, Nancy confronts the duality of her experiences—her unwavering loyalty to the Resistance tempered only by their personal cost. This complex tapestry consisted love against loss, perpetual struggle for survival and relentless search for freedom which produced mixed emotions in her life. Her memories were both burdensome and inspirations that helped in shaping the person she became over time.

What Nancy Wake experienced in her journey was a moving account of how humans could be resilient and sacrificial. In the midst of war with its everyday challenges and risks, she just kept going on. Her love for Henri, her sorrow for fallen friends, and her struggle to survive were strands of the same thread that wove the fabric of her resistance work. Throughout all these, Nancy always had a strong spirit which kept shinning amidst dark periods as a symbol of hope and bravery amid difficult circumstances.

Betrayal and Courage in the Face of Danger

In the cauldron of war, treachery and bravery often walked alongside each other, influencing Nancy Wake's path with significant consequences. The fight against the Nazis was not just a battle against external forces but also a relentless wrestling with betrayal's specters that were within oneself. Those moments when treachery occurred were more than mere tactical reversals for Nancy; they were personal tests of her mettle.

Thus, Nancy faced harsh reality with unflinching valor. In the high stakes world of French Resistance, infiltration was constantly a threat. Trust was something sacred but it could be destroyed at any given time. Betrayed by people she thought were friends, this painful experience taught her that among comrades in arms loyalty is not always assured. These slayings had personal implications for her, and all those who knew her would forever bear witness to scars left upon them.

One of the most disheartening incidents involving betrayal was from an insider whose life might have been threatened or who might have been motivated by greed to pass vital information on to Gestapo. The subsequent arrests and compromised operations represented more than merely strategic losses; they amounted to personal treacheries which endangered not only the lives of those whom Nancy had fought with but also hers. This kind of heartbreak haunted her deeply since many friends died through arrest or execution as a result of such traitorous activity.

Yet through these moments darkness Nancy still displayed remarkable courage. Instead of being hopeless after betrayals, she became resolute furthering their goals though suffering more acts of treasonous acts from those loyalists. Each act of treason strengthened this resolve and made her even more committed towards fighting for freedom and resistance movement. It wasn't only that brave people are capable to endure physical danger; they are able to confront internal upheavals caused by such perfidy as well as theirs'. Her strength lay in her ability to keep on working even when she had lost trust in humanity and it was her resilience.

Nancy's courage was not just about facing the external threats posed by the Nazis; it was about enduring the internal battles of trust and loyalty. In her world, every ally could be an enemy, every mission a risk to herself. Despite all these betrayals and dangers, Nancy never faltered, motivated by unfaltering faith in honorable causes.

Ultimately, the story of Nancy Wake's betrayal and bravery stands as a powerful reminder of the harsh realities of war. It highlights how much people must give up to resistance, but also how strong they must be to conquer such tribulations. Her journey testified subtly about how courage can overcome grave peril and unyielding human spirit that defies no matter how dark it pretends itself to be.

Daily History

Daily History

IN THE VANGARD

Organizing Key Operations

Nancy Wake's role in the French Resistance changed from being an expert operative to a remarkable leader as the war developed. This made her organization and execution of important operations vital in the fight against Nazi occupation. Her position was not simply because of her ranking, but also showed her deep commitment, strategic brilliance, and unwavering bravery.

Her leadership journey began through experiences on the ground. She realized that there was so much need for well-coordinated resistance efforts after she had observed how it worked out. When it came to leading others, her approach was that of both practicality and inspiration. She appreciated that for them to succeed, each mission had to be expressly planned and executed with her comrades' full strengths applied.

Daily History

One major task she accomplished entailed organizing sabotage missions targeting critical German infrastructure whereby sabotage operations aimed at important German infrastructure is one significant contribution Nancy made towards the struggle against occupation by Nazis sabotaged a great deal of the Nazi supply lines while disrupting their communication networks as well as transportation systems. The high value targets identified by Nancy were characterized by attacks that had maximum impact and minimal marginal support risks for their teams while planning everything meticulously such that even if these jobs were only successful they would leave the enemy disoriented and vulnerable.

Besides setting up plans and seeing them into action, Nancy went ahead with recruiting new members into the underground movement. She imparted knowledge plus skills on those who joined after her so that they became much stronger within themselves hence making their operations even more effective than before moving forward with their deeds alongside other fighters. Her ability to inspire plus motivate people played an essential part in ensuring resilience as well as morale among resistance fighters thus building allegiance amongst his followers who saw him serving this noble cause with dedication discipline required across all fields of action where danger lurked at every turn.

Among several notable activities carried out under Nancy's leadership was one which saw a German munitions depot successfully sabotaged. This mission called for close coordination and timing, as well as an in-depth understanding of enemy movements and weaknesses. A successful operation, which resulted from Nancy's leadership, thus dealt a major blow to the Germans in their war effort and it raised morale among the resistance fighters.

Nonetheless, even though she was very successful in her undertakings as a leader, there were many difficulties that Nancy had to face. The consequences of discovery and betrayal always loomed large over her every action while the cost of not delivering seemed too much too bear not taking into account how many lives might have been lost because they depended on her for safety; however despite this all being true we see that she kept calm throughout without showing any signs of panic or anxiety whatsoever such little things happening around here thus making them to look like someone who would lead with empathy plus strength such situation where everybody is afraid some won't be enough courageously which by extension meant that she was respected by those living within these areas where fear prevailed during times when everyone else thought there should be despair.

In spite of all successes made by her at work, there were various challenges faced especially when she tried leading others. It was so dangerous for her members due to

Daily History

constant threat of betrayal or being discovered hence pressure mounted on their leader as well since he had responsibility towards his team also; nonetheless what makes me feel less sorry about myself now is knowing that regardless what happened next time even though many died before my eyes only him remained unshaken; instead wanting nothing more than just continuing fighting against Nazis until we can do something about it by helping hands together achieving our goals again once everything falls apart like before then such feeling gives us hope otherwise why would anyone go through all hardships endured throughout whole period no matter how long lasts? As soon as we speak highly concerning each Descriptions: 27 other's suffering then maybe some will realize happened just now while others still won't understand what I mean.

In terms of her personal life, Nancy's leadership had its own price. She bore the weight of responsibility, lived in constant

Copyrighted Material.

danger and lost many friends. But she never gave up. Her determination remained firm as she stayed committed to their cause guided by duty and a deep belief about how important it was. Nancy Wake had a significant impact on the fight against Nazi occupation through leading the charge. French Resistance succeeded because of her organizing and executing key operations that were crucial in the struggle against Nazi occupation in France. Her exceptional courage, strategic brilliance and unflagging commitment were evident in her leadership style. As a chief leader during resistance movement Nancy's heritage serves as an ultimate reminder on how one person can change history by fighting for freedom and equality.

MAJOR MISSIONS AND MILESTONES IN FIGHTING FOR FREEDOM

Nancy Wake's name is forever ingrained in the history of the French Resistance as a symbol of bravery, strategy, and unwavering dedication. She was not only challenging German authorities through her major missions but also shaping resistance movements through critical moments in history. Each mission she embarked on was an expression of her uncommon valor and tactical skill which were part of a greater fight for independence.

One notable accomplishment by Nancy Wake was her participation in the "Destruction of the Munitions Depot" in Saint-Jean-du-Gard. This act took place with meticulous planning as it was aimed at attacking one of the most important bases supplying Germans during their occupation of France's southern section. The attack time, coordinating among different resistance cells, were some of the details that did not escape Nancy's leadership. Not only did this success put the supply line out of rhythm for Germans, but also it proved that France had fighters who could stand for themselves.

The second main mission entailed Liberation of Montelimar, a significant operation within a larger scheme to regain French territories previously captured by Germans. With its strategic importance, liberating Montelimar involved careful arrangements between different groups collaborating with allied forces. Rejuvenating the efforts from diverse quarters required Nancy to bring them together and be instrumental towards any successful operation executed within such complexity. Her command ability coupled with wise strategies facilitated precision-oriented liberation minimizing casualties while maximizing effects.

Amongst other things, another milestone that Nancy participated in is called Evacuation of Allied Soldiers As allies pushed forward many soldiers got left behind enemy lines. They were lucky because Nancy helped ensure they managed to cross back into safe areas controlled by Allies after being surrounded by enemies. It meant more than just logistic management; emotions had to be taken into account too. Numerous lives were saved following this event since the morale of the Allied forces was also boosted as well as their operational capability.

The Sabotage of German Communication Lines is another major mission which underscored Nancy's tactical genius. This was because communication channels served as a nerve centre for German military operations and that, in order to weaken resistance efforts, they had to be disturbed. In strategic locations, Nancy's group simultaneously attacked key communication installations to create chaos among Germans. Such actions were pivotal in undermining enemy effectiveness on the field and hence weakening their grip over occupied France.

Nancy Wake demonstrated during all these missions an extraordinary ability to reconcile immediate tactics with wider strategic goals of the resistance movement. Nancy Wake achieved several important milestones through her individual courage and exceptional organizational skills that were instrumental in the struggle for freedom. Her unwavering commitment to the cause she believed in despite having faced life-threatening situations always stood unchallenged.

Nancy's big missions and milestones were not mere accomplishments, but part of a larger story about resistance and liberation. Every operation she headed was a stride towards freeing France again from Nazi occupation. Her legacy as an outstanding combatant for freedom in French opposition is a remarkable demonstration of the exceptional courage and leadership skills that she demonstrated at all times.

Daily History

Nancy's Contribution to D-Day

As the massive Allied invasion of Normandy loomed ahead, Nancy Wake, was a key player in the success of D-Day; a decisive operation that would shape Europe's future. Her contributions were crucial within the intricate web of preparation and execution that led to this defining moment in World War II.

Nancy's engagement started long before the first troop landed on the beaches of Normandy. The most critical role she played was the collection and conveyance of vital intelligence. It was vital for those planning to invade Germany to have accurate information on its defenses as well as troop positions so that they could determine their lines of attack appropriately. According to information she obtained from her connections within French Resistance, Nancy learnt about enemy bunkers, areas where armies were going and how they were being supplied which helped Allies

Daily History

strategists greatly. This knowledge enabled them predict and neutralize German defenses; thus playing a significant role in ensuring that D-Day operation ended successfully.

Apart from her intelligence mission, Nancy also trained French Resistance fighters for the invasion. She knew that it would need synchronized resistance actions hence worked relentlessly to ensure all local forces were ready by the time Ally landings began. This included setting up training programs, supplying weapons among different cells apart from establishing channels through which communication could be made between these units and commanders within Allies' forces. Through these efforts she ensured that resistance had both arms while still keeping its targets aligned with broad invasion goals.

On D-day itself, Nancy refocused her energies towards giving support on ground to Allied troops who had landed. In anticipation of such landings by Allies initial attempts at sabotage operations were executed by French Resistance under her watch so as disrupt logistics for Germans thereby making communication impossible. Such undertakings played an important part in slowing down German troops' reinforcement efforts while aiding forward movement of allies with ease so as to take over enemy territories. The effectiveness of her leadership in these missions, often performed under duress and always in danger of being found out, spoke volumes for her courage and ingenuity.

Nancy's involvement did not end with the initial landings. She continued to provide strategic assistance to advancing Allied forces, assisting in organizing resistance efforts and ensuring uninterrupted communications and logistical supply. It was a period when she led from the front ensuring that the Allied momentum was maintained while speeding up liberation of France itself.

The success of D-Day served as a turning point in the course of Allied campaign resulting into eventual freedom for France and defeat of the Nazis. Nancy Wake's contributions were crucial to this triumph. Her intelligence work, preparation of the resistance, and on-the-ground support were instrumental in achieving the objectives of the invasion. This shows how exceptional she is which brought out her abilities as well as dedication; it further explains why history still has many words regarding this key moment displaying her bravery together with loyalty against freedom fighters.

Daily History

LIFE AFTER THE WAR

Transitioning from War to Peace

The global conflict's end in World War II not only brought about a new chapter for those, but it also marked the beginning of another era for those who had been heavily caught up in the struggle for freedom. The French Resistance war heroine Nancy Wake's move from wartime heroics to peacetime existence was a significant trial and an opportunity for her to start again.

Nancy faced a daunting task after the war as she tried to reintegrate herself into a world that had changed beyond recognition due to long years of conflicts. She was profoundly affected by the war and returning back to civilian life did not come easily. It was hard to undo completely its emotional and mental scars even after hostilities ended. The sense of danger every time, loss of friends, tragic choices during the war left indelible marks on her mind.

Nancy's post-war recognition and fame was one of her earliest challenges that she had to deal with upon becoming a resistance leader at some point after the war. While she was honored for being courageous and contributing, this mixture of praise from wide public sphere and media focus turned out to be double-edged blade. On the other hand, there could be no going back now because this kind of attention meant that she needed to continue fighting for what she believed in priorly but it made it more difficult for Nancy because she couldn't get used being normal anymore or simply remain private person without interference from public eyes. Instantly following World War II, Nancy primarily focused on rebuilding her personal life. She tried to reconnect with family members or friends but it came along with quite rough circumstances. Her relationships were damaged by wars while shocking experiences created difficulties whereby she struggled re-establishing previous connections which played very significant roles in her life. Nonetheless, Nancy remained strong despite these challenges since people around her appreciated her great sacrifices.

She pursued charitable and humanitarian work as well. Having been through the war, she had a lifelong ambition to assist others, especially people affected by conflicts and those who suffered from injustice. Her focus was on helping veterans and championing women's and children's rights. Nancy's post-war actions were driven by the same values of her wartime experiences which showed that she retained that same desire to make a difference in every society.

Nevertheless, since then Nancy has been grappling with the difficulties of reconciling her wartime experiences with her life after war when she became more involved in humanitarian activities. These efforts were not entirely successful because changing from a dangerous life with high stakes to normal existence was not easy at all. The thrill of purpose-laden blood that used to flow during such situations was replaced by ordinary mundane reality for civilian lifestyle. It could be challenging also for someone like Nancy Wake to adjust herself in a world where nobody dies but only wanted better personal or professional lives..

Resilience and adaptability were the hallmark of Nancy Wake's life after the war. She faced up to fame, returned to private life and remained an advocate of charity in much the same way she had done as a partisan. It wasn't easy shifting from war to peace, but Nancy's ability to create something new without neglecting her past demonstrated how strong she was. As a result, her deeds during resistance movement are still worthy of emulation while reminding the world about her great zeal for survival during trying moments that eventually led her into committed service.

Copyrighted Material.

Pursuits in Politics and Public Life

After those years of war confusion, Nancy Wake decided to venture into politics and public life with the same spirit and determination that had driven her resistance activities. This transformed a fearless warrior into an influential public figure was consistent with her efforts to make a difference but also a different challenging context where she had to swim through complicated political dynamics as well as public expectations.

Nancy's participation in politics resulted from her burning need to keep advocating for what she fought for during the time of the war. Her experiences have taught her how important is justice, equality, and human rights, things that she was determined should not just be preached but applied in politics too. She embarked on a journey of passionate reforms towards meaningful changes.

Daily History

One of Nancy's most notable endeavors was veterans' family advocacy. She used this opportunity to fight for those who lost their lives or served their countries because she herself had gone through that process before. This led to policies which made it possible for veterans receive more support services than ever before; these were designed specifically to appreciate them for their sacrifices during wars.

Moreover, another area in which Nancy stood out as an activist was women's liberation and gender equality .For many women like herself what they can do has something to say about their identity that must be recognized even more when opportunities are given. Through collaboration with others, whom she could influence helping break barriers down so that women can get job positions at any level within both private and state organizations became her priority concerning gender parity among other things. She did not stop being courageous in the battlefield fighting for

Copyrighted Material.

justice while advocating for more comprehensive society.

Public speaking and media appearances were also means through which Nancy hoped to make an impact. Since she was considered as one of the heroes from wars gave her platform hence she used it talking about key matters affecting people at large. The words bore testimony to real experiences and bore a deep sense of principle that resonated with listeners, prompting them to act. Nancy was very powerful when it came to talking with action.

In her attempts to deal with political issues and the public at large, Nancy Wake faced her fair share of problems as an outstanding figure in post-war world where situations were constantly changing. These intricacies of political landscape and public attention were yet unknown territories for her however she confronted them with the same determination and honesty that had helped her survive during wars. She remained loyal to her beliefs and true to the idea that a better future is possible for everyone across the board.

Nancy Wake's life after the war was a testimony to her resilient nature and dedication to making a change off the battlefield. Her political and public endeavors mirrored her resistance work in terms of zeal and commitment in purpose. Thus she kept on advocating, speaking out publicly, helping veterans and women thereby leaving a lasting impression that reminded people that even after the war she still had courage and determination. Her career as a public figure is actually living proof that one person can significantly transform the world or make others aspire for it too.

Honors, Awards, and Recognition

Nancy Wake's notable service during World War II and her subsequent participation in public life brought a range of honors and recognitions that demonstrated the extent to which she mattered. In fact, these were in no way an affirmation of her individual successes but rather emphasized the grave impact that she had on the course of war itself as well as its aftermath.

One of the most noteworthy accolades that Nancy received was the George Medal, bestowed by the United Kingdom. This award illustrated how brave and bold she was during her days as a fighter for France's freedom. The awarding of George Medal to civilians for acts of bravery revealed Nancy's resolute commitment together with heroic actions amidst imminent danger. It was a moment of great pride for Nancy when this recognition came because it stood for her dedication to fighting against oppression and injustice.

Moreover, French government also awarded Nancy for her contributions with some high-ranked decorations. For exceptional heroism and service during the war she received the Legion of Honour which is one among France's highest honors. This decoration though personal is an acknowledgement by France that she played a key role in their resistance movement. It represented France's appreciation of her bravery and sacrifices made toward achieving their liberation.

Apart from Legion d'Honneur, Nancy also obtained another notable French military honor called Croix de Guerre. The bestowal upon Nancy this award celebrated remarkable risks taken by her as well as displayed bravery during working trips abroad. It testified to her gallantry under fire alongside smartness even against superior force or difficulties.

Internationally too, allies could not ignore Nancy's efforts since they were recognized globally. She received Medal of Freedom from United States Government which indicated its confidence in showing unswerving faithfulness throughout allied campaign period (World War II). And Medal Of Freedom conferred on behalf of USA ranks among non-military highest civilian awards while having the resistance and freedom as its focal points.

Moreover, Nancy Wake's life was celebrated beyond military or state honors in a more personal and symbolic manner. This aspect is evident in books, documentaries and public talks that amplified her story of an extraordinary life. These portrayals ensured that her memory would remain etched on the minds of generations to come thereby allowing them to learn from her bravery as well as devotion.

The awards and distinctions received by Nancy went way beyond ceremonial gestures; they were indicatives of her truly remarkable life that influenced deeply. They were collective expressions of gratitude for her selflessness, courage, and unwavering support of liberty. Each honor observed above illustrated how she had played significant part in global developments reminding us about sustainability of all these deeds.

When she looked back on the recognition Nancy Wake received throughout her life, she took considerable pride in knowing that she had been valued and remembered for what she did. Her awards did not only denote personal achievements but rather represented the general gratitude towards her input into making the world a better place to live in. It is through such accolades that Nancy's legacy has been preserved forever since they are an enduring testament to her exceptional existence and indelible impact made upon history itself.

LATER YEARS AND DEATH

Nancy Wake, who had been a symbol of bravery in dark times, had a somewhat quieter but still profound next stage in her life when the war was over worldwide. She spent the last years of her existence thinking and retiring inside herself with all these things that were happening to her.

In the 1990s Nancy's health started to decline. Although she suffered from chronic illnesses such as strokes, she appeared to be never relenting. In 1997 she moved into the quiet surroundings of her London home after so many decades under public scrutiny and relentless advocacy in search for a tranquil environment. This retreat was not only a physical relocation but also an emotional one as she sought peace in a world forever transformed by the war experiences.

During those later years, Nancy worked through some psychological scars from her past. However, memories of danger, loss and sacrifice often coexisted with simple joys of present existence. Her thoughts on the conflict were more than mere recollections; they became painful reminders of intricate heritage left behind by this woman. These stories were just more than narratives: they were classes in valiancy, endurance and human costs of warfare.

Her demise at 98years on August 7th 2011 marked an end of era for Nancy Wake. The death hit hard both for family members and friends as well as many individuals whose lives had been impacted by hers. The tributes that followed her passing reflected the deep respect and admiration she had earned throughout her life. Former comrades joined dignitaries at Saint Lawrence Church for her funeral service in which extraordinary contributions were recognized alongside unwavering spirit.

Stories told about her along with awards given to Nancy Wake continue to attest to this fact while inspiring others even till today. Her life ranging from bold deeds during wartime up until final reflections or silence is thus considered by many as manifestation particularly about how strong human spirit can become at challenging times. Nancy's journey is an example of how one person can change the world profoundly and forever by their courage and faith.

Her passing was much more than just losing a historical figure, rather it underlined to us about sacrifices made during times of war and unending search for peace. Nancy Wake's life and legacy continue to resonate, reflecting the indomitable spirit and remarkable courage that defined her extraordinary journey.

CONCLUSION

We are now at the end of this book and as we reminisce on the life of Nancy Wake who was a remarkable woman. It is evident that her story is about bravery, determination and kindness. Nancy's life from early years in New Zealand and Australia through to her important role within the French resistance movement and beyond exemplifies this point.

Nancy Wake's incredible heroism and unwavering battle against oppression defined her existence. In World War II, she undertook acts such as leading resistance activities, outsmarting the Gestapo, and risking herself for others which were truly heroic. The calmness with which she confronted danger and handled the complexities of war with considerable acumen mirrored her deep commitment to freedom.

However, Nancy's account is not just about wartime heroism. It also tells us about what individuals go through when they experience conflict. Beneath the heroics lay a woman burdened by personal loss and haunted by painful memories; bravado aside she had lots of scars to show for all her hard work. This quiet period began with health issues leading towards an exclusive personal withdrawal from public affairs during later years of life that signified another aspect of extraordinary existence. Her strong will power expresses itself as she tries to merge contrasting values like peace which govern civilians' lives with heroism practiced in the past.

The accomplishments that Nancy Wake made during World War II are only a part of what she has done in her lifetime. They have been manifested in people influenced by Nancy Wake, causes she has stood up for and which keep her alive forever in spirit. Her involvement in veterans' affairs, fight for women rights as well as other contributions made towards public service all sprang from

Copyrighted Material.

same values that guided any work against oppressor's unfairness should be addressed squarely; everyone should have equal opportunities while striving tirelessly until such time when entire globe becomes habitable.

In considering how much impact Nancy had on others we can see that one person can make a huge difference. This woman's life was a powerful testament to the fact that an individual's bravery and conviction can shape history as well as inspire others. Her story is an invitation to us all- never to remain silent against injustice, fighting for good causes and never under-estimating our own value.

However her death in 2011 marked the end of a remarkable life which continues to exist today. Nancy Wake's story still resonates with students who are told about her brave actions and how she stood by her principles even in the face of danger. Her contribution towards liberation war across the globe and commitment to helping those who are poor up until today serves as motivation for generations yet unborn.

In conclusion, we honor Nancy Wake in this book not just for what she achieved but also because of how she faced every challenge in life. It was full of exceptional bravery and resilience, ultimately leaving behind an indelible mark on humanity. To live right, fight justice and die faithfully are valuable lessons from the existence of Nancy Wake.

In conclusion, Nancy Wake's story is an appreciation of the ability of the human mind to triumph over misfortune and have a positive impact on society. This includes the legacies she has left behind in books that tell her brave acts and persistent efforts made by many to maintain and recognize values she was known for. We must remember that it is not only in big things that show true heroism; sometimes, it can be seen in simple acts of bravery or unwavering determination to have a better world.

BIBLIOGRAPHY

Books and Memoirs

- Braddon, Russell. *Nancy Wake: The Story of a Very Brave Woman.* Sydney: Pan Macmillan, 1956.

- FitzSimons, Peter. *Nancy Wake: A Biography of Our Greatest War Heroine.* Sydney: HarperCollins, 2001.

- Wake, Nancy. *The White Mouse.* London: Macmillan, 1985.

Historical Accounts

- Atkin, Ronald. *Pillar of Fire: Dunkirk 1940.* Edinburgh: Mainstream Publishing, 1990.

- Foot, M.R.D. *SOE in France: An Account of the Work of the British*

Special Operations Executive in France 1940-1944. London: HMSO, 1966.

- Kershaw, Alex. *Avenue of Spies: A True Story of Terror, Espionage, and One American Family's Heroic Resistance in Nazi-Occupied Paris*. New York: Crown, 2015.

- Sebba, Anne. *Les Parisiennes: How the Women of Paris Lived, Loved, and Died Under Nazi Occupation*. New York: St. Martin's Press, 2016.

Articles and Journals

- Duffy, Michael. "Nancy Wake: The White Mouse." *World War II History Magazine*, May 2002.

- Marks, Leo. "Women of the SOE." *Intelligence and National Security* 6, no. 3 (1991): 503-520.

- Macintyre, Ben. "Nancy Wake: The Most Decorated Woman of the War." *The Times*, August 8, 2011.

Documentaries and Interviews

- *Nancy Wake: The White Mouse.* Directed by Mike Smith, narrated by Russell Crowe. Sydney: Australian Broadcasting Corporation, 2002.

- *Interview with Nancy Wake*, conducted by the Imperial War Museum, 1985.

Websites

- "Nancy Wake." *Australian War Memorial*. Accessed August 29, 2024. https://www.awm.gov.au/encyclopedia/wake.

- "Nancy Wake – SOE's White Mouse." *BBC History*. Accessed August 29, 2024.

https://www.bbc.co.uk/history/historic_figures/wake_nancy.shtml.

- "Nancy Wake: Wartime Spy." *The National Archives*. Accessed August 29, 2024. https://www.nationalarchives.gov.uk/education/resources/nancy-wake-wartime-spy/.

Made in United States
Troutdale, OR
12/14/2024